PETRICHOR

POEMS AND OBSERVATIONS

by
Thomas Zampino

Petrichor

Poems and Observations

by Thomas Zampino

Southern Arizona Press
Sierra Vista, Arizona

Petrichor

By Thomas Zampino

First Edition

Content Copyright © 2024 by Thomas Zampino

All rights reserved.

Except as permitted under the Copyright Act of 1976, no portion of this book may be reproduced or distributed in any form, or by any means, or stored in a database or retrieval system, without prior written permission of the author or the publisher.

Author: Thomas Zampino
Editor: Paul Gilliland
Formatting: Southern Arizona Press

Cover Artwork: Image by Andrea (AstoKo) from Pixabay
Free for use under the Pixabay Content License
and written permission from the creator

Published by Southern Arizona Press
Sierra Vista, Arizona 85635
www.SouthernArizonaPress.com

ISBN: 978-1-960038-51-7

Poetry

Pe-tri-chor

A distinctive, earthy, usually pleasant odor that is associated with rainfall especially when following a warm, dry period.

(www.merriam-webster.com)

When sky and earth meet, the storm's hypnotic brew reminds us that we are as connected to the soil as we are to each other – likely more so. The feeling evoked, indeed the revelatory smell itself, can carry us back while firmly anchoring us in the present. And we cannot help but smile

Our personal storms may not be much different. Come explore with me

Thomas Zampino

Dedication

To all those caught in a storm

Introduction

As I get further into my 30s, I've more and more had to come to terms with the many awful, rough, and painful storms that I've faced. That we all face. Some much more than others. And some much earlier than others.

But no matter when and what kind of storms we have experienced - and that we will continue to experience - words can be powerful and healing and necessary to help us get to the other side. A brighter side. With a much more pleasant *smell* - whether by speaking them or by reading them.

Tom's sensitivity and life experiences that he shares in this book help us to not feel alone and gives us a sense of connection through his well-crafted and beautiful words.

And as he writes in his poem *Words* "Words can be just enough, even when left unspoken."

– Gui Agustini, Actor, Director, and Producer

Contents

Petrichor	10
Turbulence	11
Words	12
Going First	13
Just a Little More	14
Poetry Is	15
Interpretations	16
Along the Way	17
All In, Fall In	18
Trust Yourself	19
Stormy Whether	20
Carry On	21
Beneath and Below	22
Open Up	23
Surrounded and Surrendered	24
Truly	25
Spontaneous Love	26
Cooler Breezes	27
Rusty Nails	28
Circling	29
Fixated	30
Momentum	31
Under Consideration	32
Move	33
Subsumed	34
Winter's Softening Underbelly	35

Assumptions	36
Spaces	37
Ageless	38
Tomorrow is Yesterday, Soon Enough	39
Fundamentals	40
Confrontation	41
Precise Moment	42
Winter Remix	43
Roosters and Chickens and Bears! Oh My!	44
Soundings	45
Rain	46
Embrace	47
Summer Lights, Summer Nights	48
Lens	49
While Reports of My Death	50
Full Weight	51
A Series of Firsts	52
Vulnerabilities	53
A Moment of Alchemy	54
The Books on My Shelves	55
Witness to Humanity	56
Unsolicited Advice	57
About the Author	58
Previous Works	59

Thomas Zampino

PETRICHOR

The smell of sizzling grass pushes past
   windows
shut tight to preserve the cold household
   air
as memories of youthful summers escape
only to evaporate in the morning sun.

rains later refresh the dirt,
covering everything in its wake
with an unforgettable fragrance
some call life itself

TURBULENCE

The secret of a long, fulfilled life
is undeniably complex
What causes grand emotions in one
may move another not at all
And who can claim that superior
 knowledge,
or money,
or even time
itself is necessary or sufficient?
We all know of miserable wretches
That carry humanity's prizes as burdens.
But to fail, to start over,
to oblige the pain from the whirlwinds
surrounding us
is to still love,
still forgive,
still experiment
with our generation's unabashed resistance
to death and immortality both
Turbulence just might set us free.

Thomas Zampino

WORDS

Standing on a razor's edge of words,
I am caught between darkness and light
The lyrical renderings of language
can speak to a man's tenderness or his lust –
often simultaneously

And any competent technician of the
    tongue knows how to play to the heart
while butchering the soul
Words are the instruments,
the musicians,
the conductors,
and the music all in one.

Words can bind two new friends,
words can tear old lovers apart
Words can be just enough,
even when left unspoken

GOING FIRST

One raindrop has to be the first to hit the
    ground,
giving over its fate to something bigger
    than itself

One soldier has to be the first to die
in a war he didn't start,
giving over his anger and his grief to
    eternity

One lover has to be the first to give in,
reaching out for some tentative
    reconciliation
however imperfect

Courage enough to move us first
is mostly an illusion
while our reality
is often disguised in desperation

Thomas Zampino

JUST A LITTLE MORE

Sometimes, we need just a little more

A little more time
　as we dream the night away
A little more breath
　as we race our way back home
A little more alcohol
　to help us suck up our messiest failures

Sometimes, we need a reminder
that just a little more won't cut it
even if, sometimes, it's everything

(first published in Verse-Virtual.org, February 2024)

POETRY IS

Poetry is
stubbing your toe in the middle of the
    night, cursing your head off,
and laughing at the foolishness of it all

Poetry is
running with your kids,
getting winded because you're no longer
    thirty,
and imagining yourself one day
walking them down the aisle

Poetry is
singing at the top of your lungs,
letting someone cut ahead of you in line,
and becoming the kind of lover
that would startle a romance novelist

It's all poetry –
the everyday routines,
the surprise storybook endings

Poetry is just like that
Poetry just is

INTERPRETATIONS

Some look for the hidden meaning behind words while others take them at face value

The difference is either a reflection of our upbringing or a corresponding need to rebel

Some use technical jargon as a barrier to the entry into their club, whether consciously or not

But even the language of love is more complicated than necessary when protecting the heart

And the poet himself is no stranger to this spectacle, with layers of interpretations rationalized yet often little contemplated

It seems the older I get the more I understand that the words we embrace strip away much more than just our self-delusions

ALONG THE WAY

Bright lights from the oncoming traffic
blind me for a moment.
As my eyes adjust,
the surrounding fields come into view
and I find myself both delighted and
   solemn from a glimpse of the dairy cows
late coming back to the barn.
Spared of a faithless slaughter,
their lives of service
remind me of my own
with mindless rituals.
And a thriving depletion
along the way

ALL IN, FALL IN

Cool, wet mornings make way for cold, damp nights
wool sweaters dug out of creaky bottom drawers
and spring blankets exchanged for their winter counterparts
The ground prepares to suspend its lifeblood
But confident of its return in the months just ahead
leisurely rejuvenating, rearranging, resetting, and preparing
The crackling of crushed leaves
a stark reminder that all is nourishment for the generation soon upon us

TRUST YOURSELF

Trust yourself
like the earth anticipates the healing rain

Trust yourself
like the body knows when to let go

There is no weakness in accommodation,
no reprimand for escaping the unknown,
just a simple way forward
even when clarity seems to fail us,
even when we wish it weren't so.

Trust yourself

STORMY WHETHER

I find myself opening up to vulnerability
    much like a surgeon cutting into his own
    chest, reaching deep, massaging his
    dying muscle back to life

With every flicker, with every next breath,
    another hope, another chance, to
    reconnect, to be reminded, to ultimately
    forget – all in equal measure

I've always hated the storm but welcome
    its familiarity, its peculiar comforts,
    trusting that my next steps can be
    guided more by humility than by ego –

a satisfying, if not delusional trust, always
    there for me

even when I'm not

CARRY ON

The darkness carries its own light, one that
 feels withheld but is neither long denied
 nor far off indentured

The mind carries its own vision, one that
 seems real but is neither natural born
 nor rashly conceived

The soul carries its own heaviness, one that
 seeks true measurement but is neither
 roughly discoverable nor even sensually
 balanced

Thomas Zampino

BENEATH AND BELOW

Listen to the silence
    just below the chaos
Look to the space
    just beneath the mess
For peace is still a goal to be pursued
    not wished for
And the jaded heart ever fails to be
    set free

OPEN UP

Closed mouth, closed eyes, closed mind
as if the body and soul remain boundless
without renewal without second chances
as if nothingness itself danced alone

Thomas Zampino

SURROUNDED AND SURRENDERED

In simplest terms, I have found my
   purpose
Not that you can tell from my everyday life
where I'm surrounded by the pre-anxieties
and the post-complexities of a work-life
balance that I am constantly losing
To the dual contrivances of shame
And duress.

But look closely and watch
as I surrender to the inevitable
(and the finality)
of a bare-bones orthodoxy one more time

TRULY

Life increases for those who understand
 that every hour carries with it a
 desperate certainty to educate

– if only we truly understood time

Humanity appears to those who believe
 that every action carries with it one
 moment of clarity before the ego takes
 hold

– if only we truly understood self

Souls grasp nothing from earlier
 generations, each remaining complicit in
 its own defeat

– if only we truly understood death

Thomas Zampino

SPONTANEOUS LOVE

Was it your fierce brown eyes that first drew me in?
ready to pounce on every shadow real or imagined
Or was it in the uncomplicated parting of your lips?
embracing, in turn, melancholy and inquisitiveness
Unlike the sun, I will set aside the better part of the
years still ahead only to draw upon the abundance
                when the light begins to die

COOLER BREEZES

The sticky, hot summer winds are escaping
   towards the south
replaced by the colder Canadian air that's
   making itself known
I'm neither bothered nor sad about the
   conclusion of summer
because early fall's cooler breezes fit my
   personality so much better.
Sweaters and hats and open windows
   that mean I can
better catch the sing-song lullabies of the
   visitors in the yard
the ones that will fast be hitching a ride
   along with the winds
escaping towards the south. Bring it on, old
   man, bring it on.

RUSTY NAILS
Remembering My Dad

They are still usable, these rusty nails that I
   found in a bucket
in my dad's basement. Hundreds of them.
   Along with tools
of every size and shape imaginable. Some
   still in their original
packaging. Others left for me to guess at
   their usefulness
But I kept coming back to look at those
   nails, to smell the rust
to feel their steely sharpness some thirty or
   even forty years
packed tightly together, impenetrable
   except for the moisture
surrounding us. I like their tenacity, their
   ability to hold back
time with their orange and brown covering
   easily scrapped off
only then to reveal their readiness for the
   next available job

CIRCLING

It's easier to find yourself unprepared for
    the next obvious gift
than to fix your eyes, your head, your
    frightening lack of guile
on your failures and fornications
Step up my boy and begin to act on your
    talents and hopes
dreaming the biggest dreams, slaying the
    ugliest of dragons
tasting first of death before living

FIXATED

Imagine, like any beast, we were fixated on
    the present moment
aware of the past but as untroubled by
    yesterday's failures as
we were unconcerned about tomorrow's
    unavoidable affairs.
A deep preoccupation with life's sights,
    sounds, and smells
now a cold tonic for the alienation and
    hubris of humanity
thereby insulting death with our
    unflagging pretenses

MOMENTUM

Once an attempt is made, it's impossible to
 start over again as if nothing changed
but that's the sublime operation of
 momentum
Every movement, every turn, every step
 forward, compels some new choice that
might not have been contemplated in
 advance
but becomes indistinguishable from the
 inevitable looking back from the depths
of our life, our loves, our tears, and our
 laughter

Thomas Zampino

UNDER CONSIDERATION

The faster I head towards the dark, damp
    earth, the lighter my days feel
but the truth lies somewhere between my
    reality and my imagination
even if both openly deceive me
I arrived here without desire to live
    forever (not that I was given a choice)
but find myself, from time to time, acting
    the fool pretending that I did
even if most of me understands

MOVE

This old car once needed only the
    occasional tune up to keep it running
for the few neighborhood trips that were
    sparingly planned. Thinking
about the day ahead, I reach for a coffee –
    a list of chores in hand
that has only grown longer since yesterday.
    But right now only
one really matters. And that piston slap
    keeps reminding
me to pick up the pace lest I spend all of
    my time complaining

Thomas Zampino

SUBSUMED

The man I once was still exists, living on
    mostly in my head now
the purpose, the sharpness, the glorious
    virility race just ahead
except when I stop, as I more often do, to
    take inventory, to look
outside of myself a little more closely, to
    feel astonishment from
the smallest of miracles that once went
    unnoticed or untouched
I happily tip my hat and wish him well,
    knowing that the faster he
advances, the sooner he'll catch up to me
    while I sit here, waiting

WINTER'S SOFTENING UNDERBELLY

The early morning darkness gives way to
    winter's softening underbelly
The temperature rises throughout the day,
    falling back quickly at dusk
Here and there a gentle hint of life
    recalibrating just below the surface
While the leaf buds are slowly, delicately
    sniffing at the air to ferret out
The exact right moment to coordinate their
    elegant and giddy swagger

Thomas Zampino

ASSUMPTIONS

The sun pretends that spring is fast
    approaching
while the snapdragons call late winter's
    bluff
the damp, dark ground assessing that the
greater risk lies in failing to gather up
the day than in assuming death is
waiting just around the corner

SPACES

The silence between the notes
The earth between the flowers
The hours between the storms
These are the naked spaces
where we embody the fullness
of life's most precious gifts

AGELESS

There is nothing inevitable about getting
   older
some maintain a youthful vigor through
   endless physical effort
some exercise brain cells until their heads
   explode with knowledge
and some just sit quietly, hoping that
   infirmity and sickness might pass by
if they don't wave any red flags that draw
   attention to their passivity and fears.
But the mind will have none of it insisting,
   as it does, on stepping into some bland
   reality –
one that informs the heart that we exist,
   ageless and far beyond all that we have
   ever seen.
Even the body seems to know

TOMORROW IS YESTERDAY, SOON ENOUGH

Sorting through another stack of
 photographs to be digitized
I'm stuck on the thought of how much has
 changed, as if my
earlier life were some made up story of
 toddlers learning to
walk, dance and piano recitals, homework,
 screams of glee
tears of loss, and always, always
 monumental struggles over
finding the right words to say – being
 empathetic yet holding
back just enough to encourage those hints
 of independence
that every parent recognizes but
 sometimes fails to see
These photographs are concrete reminders
 that tomorrow is
yesterday, soon enough

FUNDAMENTALS

Developing theories to understand the
 world is both time consuming and futile
Science seeks to impose rationality on a
 chaotic world but often stumbles with
 each new discovery
Religion, too, can spook us into irrational
 judgments far afield from ancient truths,
 thereby destroying our common bonds
And while the social sciences can attempt
 to characterize human nature, their
 governing assumptions often lead to
 even greater conflict
It's as if there is some hidden hand that
 permits only so much knowledge at one
 time lest we become both overwhelmed
 and unnecessarily afraid
Yet the fundamentals always seem to
 prevail: to love much, to seek the good,
 to sacrifice willingly, to raise our voices
 to the heavens in supplication and
 thanks
These remain humanity's great
 generational gifts to itself

CONFRONTATION
On War and Fighting Back

Subtle at first, like a cat burglar pouncing in the night: taking things, breaking things – mostly unnoticed until it was too late
Then a sudden, quick swerve in broad daylight: breaking people, taking people – mostly indifference until the battle was joined
Then all hell was loosened, blood libels pandered to, victims drowned in a sea of false accusations. Again
Your transactional concerns for a people highlighted by years of malfeasance – no, by your very obvious contempt. Again
They are pawns in a game of global destruction, cynically packaged in the pitiful name of world peace. Again
– Never again –

Thomas Zampino

PRECISE MOMENT

There is a precise moment that
separates day from night
inhalation from exhalation
life from death
It is within that space
where there exists
neither boundary nor border
that the eternal becomes the present
and the present disappears
There, we will find each other

(originally published in *Precise Moment*)

WINTER REMIX
A Haiku

Winter's glacial slap
A swift reshuffling of time
Between north and south

Thomas Zampino

ROOSTERS AND CHICKENS AND BEARS! OH MY!

Secluded in a little mountain hideaway in rural Pennsylvania,
the weather is perfect, chilled but not frozen, and the twigs
crunch beneath our feet on a several mile hike in the woods.
Our guide lives off the land, hunting, fishing & chopping trees
building things for his family, a wife and twin 13 year olds who
are learning skill sets so appropriately different than my own.
It's peaceful here and actually quite luxurious and abundant
for a place in the woods – with the sounds of roosters and
chickens, the rustling of leaves, and a bear or two spotted
recently (iPhone photographic proof courtesy of our guide)
A happy place to be while remembering 37 years together

SOUNDINGS

Whether bounded by water or by air, a desperation for
clarity can overwhelm even the most hard nosed
among us, pretending all the while that none of
it really matters – a dialectical discourse made for one?

RAIN

Punishing the windowpane before soaking
    the soil,
the often violent ride from cloud cover to
    groundswell
I count among the miracles for which we
    no longer have
either goodwill or patience. But miracles
    need no validation
from us to justify their existence

EMBRACE

It's not as if every heartbeat embraces its
    true nature
this unthinking, habitual routine unwinds
    itself over time
but is always present in the moment,
    neither future nor past
challenging its innocence or some yet
    uncharted vulnerability.
One measure of time reminding us that
    trust is often disguised as
a deep, incomprehensible silence

Thomas Zampino

SUMMER LIGHTS, SUMMER NIGHTS

Every minute of daylight shields the body
from laboring against the dank dark night
when demons of our own making inhabit
the head and push back against the soul
but as luck would have it, even the night
can take us back to the beginning, reset
the clock, and compel the mind to wake
... this, the stuff of summer

LENS

you convince yourself that your urgencies,
    your provocations, your desperation
entitle you to stand before generations past
    and cry out now in anguish, as
if you are unique, separate, distinguishable
    from the souls preceding you.
dis-ease, dis-information, dis-order persist
    – the very currency of history,
never content to settle down, always
    prepared to mock our most obnoxious
pretensions. Fear is not only a tool best
    suited to incite change, it's
also a catalyst, one all too eager to swap
    out the living for the
dead as soon as our unspoken memories
    fail us

Thomas Zampino

WHILE REPORTS OF MY DEATH

are greatly exaggerated, they are only a tad
   early
I'm not talking about anything around the
   corner
just a deeper recognition that the number
   of
daily affairs once considered incalculable
were in fact numbered at birth. But
fear is not the same as panic
and numbers remain
illusions even after
they're counted

FULL WEIGHT

I want you to always see me, I want you to
    always feel me next to you
even when we cannot be physically close by
    – distance is an illusion
I want you to know I am here, that you are
    fully present in my heart
not as two parts aligned as one, but two
    measures of equal force
guiding the loving hands of a daily re-
    creation, beginning anew,
joining each other with the full weight of
    our existence

A SERIES OF FIRSTS

First breath, first cry – demanding the
　　world yet completely dependent
First crawl, first walk – annexing strength
　　for arms then legs then mind
First date, first mate, first job –
　　strategizing and jockeying for position
First child, first lessons, first blunders –
　　knowing just too damn little
First acceptance, first release, first insights
　　– gaining by relenting
First attempts to start over – even if
　　nothing would be different

VULNERABILITIES

As guys go, my vulnerabilities are more or less kept in check
Hidden on the outside, whatever feelings may have registered on the inside
Patriarchal strength, once touted if not prized, is still anticipated on some level
If only inside my own head, pushing through absent-minded generational demands
But expectations have a way of softening over time, one part of the letting go process
I think I'm right on schedule

Thomas Zampino

A MOMENT OF ALCHEMY

A moment of alchemy slipped in between
 us
as we circled in rhythm for the first time
even with awkward feet still learning.
A turn, a smile, a waltz, a blur. The
room behind us disappearing.
Two of us, transported
somewhere outside.
But then landing
safely. Just in
time.

(previously published in *synchronicity*)

THE BOOKS ON MY SHELVES

I haven't read them all and likely never will
 in this lifetime
The colors, sizes, and titles are just so
 compelling on my wall
even if they are more of a testament to
 abundance than education
But it doesn't matter as I'm still more
 inclined to pick one off the shelves
to thumb through it for some randomized
 facts than to search an e-reader
The heft, the smell, the leisurely turn of a
 page, all trigger old sensory memories
The physical and the mental intertwined
 forever in the dance of words upon
 paper

Thomas Zampino

WITNESS TO HUMANITY

Sometimes all we can do is watch in horror
   or fascination
Sometimes we can only listen offering our
   silence as a gift
We've all been there, the drama, the
   trauma, the enduring pain
looking for a way out and even, on
   occasion,
familiar touchstones that remind us that
   our fear and loathing
are often more necessary than real
That's the thing about privilege
we get to witness humanity and
sometimes just return the favor

UNSOLICITED ADVICE

You aren't so much what you eat as you are
    what eats at you
It's ok, sometimes, to "be that guy" if that
    guy is who you are
Today is the first day of the rest of your life
    but so is tomorrow
The person who lights up a room also
    carries many darker days
Want more unsolicited advice?
Never take unsolicited advice from anyone
Including me

Thomas Zampino

About the Author

Thomas Zampino lives in New York and has been an attorney for nearly 40 years. He began writing poetry only recently. His work has appeared in The University of Chicago's *Memoryhouse Magazine, Silver Birch Press, Bard's Annual 2019, 2020, 2021, 2022,* and *2023, Trees in a Garden of Ashes, Otherwise Engaged, Chaos, A Poetry Vortex, Nassau County Voices in Verse, No Distance Between Us,* and *The Wonders of Winter*. His first book of poetry, *Precise Moment*, was published in 2021 and Brazilian producer, director, and actor Gui Agustini produced a video enactment of his poem *Precise Moment*.

His second book, *synchronicity,* was published in 2023 by Southern Arizona Press.

He can be followed at:

https://thomaszampino.wordpress.com/

Previous Works

After nearly 40 years as a corporate and property tax attorney in New York City, Thomas Zampino's poems just about popped into existence at the **Precise Moment** when they could no longer be held back. This is a broad selection of mostly simple observations about life, faith, and meaning as seen through the eyes of someone who was profoundly touched by the world around him long before he realized it. Influenced by American poet Billy Collins and English poet David Whyte, these poems are a reflection of the aging - and hopefully the maturing - process in real time.

https://www.blurb.com/b/10812828-precise-moment-pb

In this, his second book of poetry, Thomas Zampino imparts flashes of intimacy, intensity, and inevitableness. At its core **synchronicity** can be read as a love story. One not only existing between lovers, but one that also reveals how synchronicity - seemingly unconnected moments of "coincidences" - lovingly shaped a life fully lived. A lifetime of poetry observed, told without pretense or presumption.

https://www.amazon.com/dp/1960038028

Made in the USA
Middletown, DE
29 March 2024